OF COURSE,

OF COURSE,

Poems by

Allen Tice

© 2021 Allen Tice. All rights reserved.
This material may not be reproduced in any form, published,
reprinted, recorded, performed, broadcast,
rewritten or redistributed without
the explicit permission of Allen Tice.
All such actions are strictly prohibited by law.

Cover art by Maryellen Tice

ISBN: 978-1-63980-016-2

Kelsay Books
502 South 1040 East, A-119
American Fork, Utah 84003
Kelsaybooks.com

To my family and my Latin teacher Mme. Cecil W. Cantrell

Acknowledgments

Arion: "Very Late, In Spring" [PMG 976]
Blue Unicorn: "Pals at the Barn Dance,"
    "A Motion for Leave to Appeal,"
    "While Walking the Delectable Mountains"
Bumbershoot: "And at the Writers Conference"
Gamut: "Spoken at the Square Dance"
Leviathan Quarterly: "Applying the Axiom of Choice,"
    "Sonnet to Orpheus 1,9"
Light Quarterly: "Basho's Foghorn,"
    "Boost Repeat Sales with Dactylic Studies,"
Lucid Rhythms: "Happy Birthday!"
The Classical Outlook: "People from Leros,"
    "The Mannequins"
The New Republic: "He Pictures the Brevity of His Own Life,
    and How Nothing Seems to Have Lived"
The New York Times: "The Greenmarket"
The *News* of the *Classical Association:* "Let's Live!"
    "*Carmina* of Horace, Book I, Number 5,"
    "To a Sea Captain Dining at Ease with His Hostess —
        Ψαπφω 31" [Sappho],
    "After Sappho, Fragments 105a and 105c,"
    "A Roman Poet Remembers Pompeii & Herculaneum"
    "Very Late, In Spring" [PMG 976] (earlier version)
The Raintown Review: "I Packed Some Lunch, You Know,"
    "Take This Rose"
Think Magazine: "Goalie"
Trinacria: "Woman: Cubiculum, House VI, 15, 14, Pompeii,"
    "By the Meistersinger,"
    "Tabletop Thoughts,"
    "Full Moon, Santorini"
Umbrella: "A Gathering with Horace"
[Willard Espy's] *The Word's Gotten Out:*
    "Spoken at the Square Dance"

Extra Thanks

In addition to the dedicatees mentioned earlier, I want to thank many friends and critiquers on Eratosphere who are too many to mention, some of whom gave important help with the deepest connotations in early Greek and Latin. There are also those who might have popped a good idea into my head somehow but whose help must inevitably remain largely unacknowledged: the trees, the sky, the random artificers of reality at the right moment. And, of course, other close relatives who tolerated my scribbles.

Contents

At a Guest House on the Outskirts

At a Guest House on the Outskirts	15
Anne Bradstreet's Motto for Today	16
Cippus	17
Small Do at "Domatia Mou" in Kavala, Greece, 2008	18
To Homer They Were Talking Flowers	19
PolyAnna	20
An Ordinary Day	21
Tinkling Bells and Sounding Buoys	22
A Gathering with Horace ~ 10 BC	23
Headwind	24
Into the Million Pavilion	25
Urban Rainfall	26
Of April That It Is, and So the Year	27
Near an Exceptional Bookstore	28
I Packed Some Lunch, You Know	29
Happy Birthday!	30
A Motion for Leave to Appeal	31
Belle of the Ball	32
Pals at the Barn Dance	34
Wisconsin Rhapsody	35
In the Mood	36
Strolling Around	37

Bolero

Summer Moon on Calm Water	41
Full Moon, Santorini	42
The Plague, A.D. 2020	43
For Rembrandt's Landlord, Christoffer Thijsz	44
Quick	45

Bolero, Say Hello—Nobody Is Exactly Like Toots	46
The Big Carpet	48
Boost Repeat Sales with Dactylic Studies	49
Tabletop Thoughts	50
More Golden than Gold	51
Basho's Foghorn	52
Capriccioso	53
Winter Full Moon	54
Take This Rose	55
Woman: Cubiculum, House VI, 15, 14, Pompeii	56
If They Want a Reason, Invite Them Too!	57
Song for the Grand Ole Opry—It Never Happened	58
Goalie	59
Apple Tree Lean Down	60

At the Square Dance

After *Lecto compositus* of Petronius Arbiter	63
At a Café Nervosa Reading on Cornelia Street	64
And at the Writers Conference,	65
The Earthquake and Magnetism Man	67
Tanglewood	69
The Greenmarket	70
Spoken at the Square Dance	71
Analogue Beauty	72
Survivors' Club	73
A Wedgwood Vase	78
Bronx Cheer	79
Disembarking at the Poem Station	80
Applying the Axiom of Choice	81
Einstein at Princeton Reflects on the Earlier Music of France	82

What the Trees Told Me to Say	83
Sum summus mus. ("I am the mightiest mouse."	
—Latin, anonymous)	84
While Walking the Delectable Mountains	85
The Number Bird	86

Literary Translations

Carmina of Horace, Book I, Number 5	89
Very Late, in Spring	90
To a Sea Captain Dining at Ease with His Hostess	91
Let's Live!	92
After Sappho, Fragments 105a and 105c	93
A Roman Poet Describes Pompeii &	
Herculaneum	94
By the Meistersinger	95
A Father Speaks to Confucius:	
LunYu 1: 1; 11:26, 27	96
The Olfactory Organ	97
He Pictures the Brevity of His Own Life, and	
How Nothing Seems to Have Lived	98
People from Leros	100
The Mannequins	101
Pennsylvania Dutch Children's Prayer	102

At a Guest House on the Outskirts

At a Guest House on the Outskirts

At a guest house I raid where they
Stow caffeine and easy sodas. Sipping
A microwaved coffee, I imagine a man
Exhausted on the shores of Cavafy—he who
Made silver moments gleam like blue
Tintinnabula played in the morning distance,
Yet very nearby, while a chanticleer calls.

That man becomes me again, though at a farm,
Living in two worlds at once, watching my
Books march on their shelf while fireflies
Blink outside. The farm is small, the world
Is small. Even today's farm house where
Another coffee steams is only large enough
For a few. Let me tell you this story.

Anne Bradstreet's Motto for Today

Increase my strengths.
Help my heart to shelter households.
Grace my griefs with good news of spring.
Lead me to words that work well for the weary.
Hide my faults from the foolish.
Look long into me and teach me.
Drive off needless fear.
Let me nourish the young with wisdom and conscience.
Repair my mistakes if I forget my footing.
Bring peace as possible and help people be mindful.
Increase my good.

Cippus

He knew what he liked, so after he gave Geppetto the
Preserved kabuki, the visitor strode from the House of the
Translators over a bridge to where he examined a cippus of
Poems carved in an inflected language, where the author had
Taken pains to hide the sex of all the pronouns (a minor feat
Considering their rhythms) in more than one text. Yet, in all
The different tourist kiosk versions, these subtle poems had
Sprung a nonexistent gender.

All the translators, that is, except for the greatest one, who,
In a note, carefully pointed out the cover-up for a single
Dedication (yet who did not discuss those other poems).
Formidable translator, though actually a bit more than that.
The visitor liked reading the plinth in the sunlight.

From the open bookshop door by the kiosk, a melodious
FM radio soprano gnome was singing, "They'll figure it out,"
Blah-blah, "They'll figure it out," over and over. Yet,
What perfect and subtle taste by that astonishing author.
What an exquisite language. What an expert poet.

Small Do at "Domatia Mou" in Kavala, Greece, 2008

Some swallows have nests by our window,
The dining room's under repair,
The taxis are redder than ketchup,
There's five kinds of love in the air.

Our ferry will plow soon for Lesvos,
The car rental shop is our friend,
We'll be staying at Sappho's Eressos,
Watching the moon at land's end.

There's no place like home says the proverb,
Though it's thousands of years in the past.
The music of Greece is fantastic,
It's good to be back here at last.

To Homer They Were Talking Flowers

(Neotibicen Auletes)

The sometime silence rings as if you or I
Had heard it from those faraway homes we knew
  Long years ago when we were only
    Children amazed at a hint of music.

Now through the greenery on the heated miles
Rumpling beyond our carefully shadowed quilt,
  Gold honeybees dart quietly, as
    Butterflies wobble in lazy zigzags

And many-voiced cicadas approve the sun's
Shrill fire aloud with rhythms of castanets,
  Strumming, like tree-top kings that chatter
    Endlessly delicate busy speeches.

The twinkling hum that purls along trees and roads—
Stillness abuzz with murmurous sudden whirrs—
  Slows time and woos the sun from rolling
    Further, while smiles and our cups of wine fill,

Releasing small jokes into the summer skies.
A book of verse, the wilderness, you and I!
  Let's picnic, while these wild cicadas
    Surge in their giddiness and we listen.

PolyAnna

The waitress at the Metropole Café
Spoke Polish with her eyes, and walked in Greek
With feet that were entirely built in France
On shoes of fine Italian leather under
Subtle Japanese, as was the dance
Behind the menu. What language did she speak?
Sometimes English. Sometimes, I couldn't say.

An Ordinary Day

Night swings zodiac stars far above Denver's stairs
While blue vanishes. Stark mountains make sharp parade.
Burnt gold drops off the bright peaks,
Car lights rise out of valley shade,

And I'm tipsy with your molecules close to me,
And your touch is a sure marvel beyond all test,
While all twilight we ramble
Until silence lays doubt to rest.

You must hear what I say. Nothing on earth reveals
Grace more fully than you there in an evening gown
All as lovely as those hills
Folding upward around this town.

Our lives tumble about, strolling on precious rugs,
Flagstones, wading to stampedes of the human heart—
Here, each word is a gesture,
There, dawn bells light a world apart.

Not one woman exceeds what she was given, though
Each man thinks he is God's specialty. Look at you!
A magnificent rose bud
Beside nettles, where all have thorns.

How your laughter, alight with unforgettable
Regard I don't deserve, puts all my acts in tune.
Ah well now, if you say even
One more word, I might paint the moon.

Tinkling Bells and Sounding Buoys

Fair in the sunset, fairer than rainfall,
Motions more lovely than gingham in air
Billowed at evening beside shaded windows,
    Amuse-bouche of lemons.

Unseen horizons tilt pathways apart,
Scattershot gravel spun in rat-a-tat hail,
Gondolas step slow as silk flown on water,
    Rose lettered echoes.

Porcelain songbirds awink, feathery boas—
Tinsel tree blossoms. Weather's slow turning.
Excellent fiasco, ha! Despair's blue earthquake.
    Those passed, the seasons.

Talk from afar. Click of hurrying footsteps.
Trifles and gossip above coffee and toast.
Fond time is yet wonderful. Always you
    Demonstrate moonlight.

A Gathering with Horace ~ 10 BC

   Look, how over the grape arbors, Augustus, those
Cloud heaps float to the world's edges like woolly fleeces
Piled up, airy, indifferent
To poets as to minotaurs.

   Twilight pours from the gold mirror beyond the west,
Soft Greek melodies drift under the torches. Ah—
They call: Time for those few words!
Our friends rise to applaud your health.

   Togas talk till your birthday celebration's done—
Then we're here, just a bit drunk in the country dark,
Numbering stars—as indifferent
To Homer as to ancient seas.

Headwind

Six planets are in retrograde today
And Venus hides from Mercury beyond
The sun. I'm mountaineering on the level
Street to: 'Let your hair down after dark,
There is no other. Look, I am not bevel,
Nor lives there any different one so fond
As when I thought of rings and words to say,

"Bring on the planets' merry disarray,
With our short lives and images that fool,
Or vacant thoughts that lovers are like soups,
With flavors each their own." When cutty sark
Is served, when prince and princess loop the loops,
My simple compass is your golden rule.'
Let threats to friendships scatter where they may.

Into the Million Pavilion

Descending to the airport from above—
On interurban rail or by car—
From thirty, maybe fifty miles away,

Unasked, a silent clarion can rise
To him that says, "Hello, you're back. Please stay.
I missed you badly, annoying though you are."
It's like a woman's fragrance he could love.

What bells are these among the rumors there?
He's felt them on the highway several times,

Quiet as a sunup. A thought that knows
Exactly who he is, knows him by eyes
And choice, and wonders what he might propose.

They're such a welcome welcome, these tiny rhymes
From no one. Oh what's the drama? Why this care?

Urban Rainfall

It's raining and
I've turned out the lights
with this window open
to watch it pour down
like my grandparents did.

It's quiet
with the fragrance of rain.

The only thing
not artifact
is the sky.

Of April That It Is, and So the Year

A lovely lady on a lawn, more fair
than wakeling birds that chant in trees at dawn—
or pushing Eden-spare through curtained leaves—
surprises me at times when half-awake.
She has a dozen names, and all are yours,
and moods that call from centuries far gone,
as when Philippa tidied Chaucer's hair.

Near an Exceptional Bookstore

Not many-minded Mozart, nor the bronze
of Caesar's legions could turn me from these
boulevards, swift with traffic, or night's stupendous
and stunning nocturnal regions. The moon is rising
pink as dawn. Deep groves hum. Cars blur through
shapes of park and green. Let down to me your silk
hair, and we can all the pleasures approve
of grocery carts, champagne waltzes, Keats and Yeats,
or Gymnopédies on the limo radio at the curb lane.

Let me dive through your faithful metro
that bounces below the Milky Way to rise
in a sudden slow thundering express runaway up hill.
Let me paint pictures of you at sunrise across the clouds
looking out toward all the world while harmonies of Bach
permeate the rolling stock downstairs—
*Times Square station! Change for Parthenon to Colosseum
and Luna Central, Barnard's Star*—now,
Swerve the hammered wheels. Here's the platform:

By our whirling globe and the winds of every quarter,
my thirst for you is as sharp as moonlight, and Bach's
great Fugues leap the distances from earth to heaven.
I feel your heart move. I have a stereo of Bach—

Not many-minded Mozart, nor Caesar's legions
can turn me from your murmurs or these
stupendous and stunning nocturnal regions.

  It is dark now. Let down to me your hair,
  step down every stair tonight,
    where by a bower below your tower
      praising the hour, I write.

I Packed Some Lunch, You Know

Late beach, as far waves rammed an Atlantic coast,
Blood hot I felt your weight on the humid air
And thought I heard your sandals shifting
Softly beside me and turned; you weren't there.

Today we explore Lake Ontario's shoreline and
Spot sailing birds, far off in the summer air.
Their darts delight us watchers below.
Little is happening. The world is stock-still.

Could those be wild grapes? Close in that spinney hides
A shadowed leaf-filled cluster, alive and sweet.
The weather-wise bees lunge in by-ways,
Trembling the countryside's afternoon heat.

Yet see how time's least butterfly waits upon
This limb, unfolding, folding with perfect wing-
Beats ballerina lifts for our eyes,
Making us glad like a childhood plaything.

Beguiled, I find touchstones for a winding path
To rosebuds, stray past cupolas, mistletoe,
Cool maples. Great anthems of silence
Jealously shelter our quiet hello.

There, look, those far off clouds of this simple day
Could drum with rain. Meanwhile, here are petals small
That touch like gold dust oiled in warm spice.
Everything's happening. No one will fall.

Happy Birthday!

Aware of silver labyrinths in blossoms,
the traveler buys a corsage and a rose
in a simple garland and no one stares.
The flowers are gratified, we may suppose:
at least they bowl along electric airs,
full unencumbered by midnight sun,
perfusing resistless beauty everywhere,
as pilgrim, walking with quiet sense,
steps back to zooming home once more,
cooling and calming with happy noise,
speeding again love's busy heart.

A Motion for Leave to Appeal

No barrister, I sue as I discover
My cause to try at love's most favored court:
Where summons is not blind to beauty's lawyer,
Citing love's views where law's decrees fall short.
Deny my claim, I counsel my distress.
Enjoin, disclose, or help in my defense.
Postpone no pleas nor stay beyond redress,
Full jurisprudence embodies evidence.
Endorse a licensed act on your behalf,
Then I'll search lover's title to the deed
Until law's uses lapse, and then we laugh,
Adjourning to chambers in deliberate speed,
To ponder there and cite with due process
The proof of law in love's all loveliness.

Belle of the Ball

I'd like to dance with you,
Wander in France with you,
Apply for grants with you,
Buy garden plants with you,
Take a big chance with you,
Go the distance with you,
Defy some cant's with you,
Do a swan dive with you.

I want to prance with you,
Live in a manse with you,
Sing solemn chants with you
Dare an advance with you,
Wear formal pants for you,
Make an entrance with you,
Shock all our aunts with you,
Have a nice drive with you.

I want to glance at you,
Never askance at you,
Enter a trance with you,
Juggle finance with you,
Extravagance with you,
Walk on my hands for you,
Slyly contrive with you.
Cook an endive with you.

Let me romance with you,
Twist a nuance with you,
Do gallivants with you,
Engage in rants with you,

Do brain implants with you,
Save elephants with you,
Just be alive with you.
I want to dance with you.

Pals at the Barn Dance

If I were you or you were I, my friend,
You dreaming me, I holding your own court
In your deep rooms, with matchless muses rare
Thundering 'round—pleasing the ears I'd lend—
To lift my views with wholesome tidbits fair
And balanced, ah! while unaware, in short,
Of one now near though very much apart,
Who dreams he were great 'me'—with my delights—
And I had his more secondary rights;
Well, would I trade forever? You know my heart.
It has not changed, not like a weary flower.
I'd laud you there, as here—yet can you guess
The happiness you waste costs far, far less
Than what I taste, sober beyond this hour.

Wisconsin Rhapsody

He likes to see his lovely lassy there
In Madison, Wisconsin's Greyhound station —
Alive at the planet's best encounter, filling
Those coffee cups he needs to be serene —
Far from the bus announcer's clarion shrilling,
Her recreation serving dawn flirtation
Like easy sunrise. So, what does he declare?

Oh, listen to my words. He just remakes
Mountains from soda fountains, billets-doux
From luncheonette placemats, while he devours
Waffles drowned in syrup and apple yogurt,
And groans about the earliness of her hours,
Then leaves a *pourboire* on the breakfast menu
That rests beside the showcase full of cakes.

In the Mood

Trim round loquacious volumes of roasty words
That swan about side step with a dancing eye....
  My love, you're a round, right rose so near. Ha,
  Let me persuade you like something awesome!

Then run afoot, that doorway, the curtain whirl,
Outside, and kiss me long while the music pours
  (It sways) before they catch on we're gone
  Down—through the night, in the dark, away.

Strolling Around

A song without a lot of sense, for fun.
An ode to let the sunset roll around.
A little leisure for a walk
Below the evening glimmer.

A verse as easy as a picnic snack
Outdoors among the people that we greet.
Some thoughts that barely have a point.
My hat's a flaxen skimmer.

And there's a pretty little yacht in blue
Afloat on waters that are also blue.
The moon is rising fat and gold,
Improving my libido.

The boat is turning toward a landing now.
I think I see their faces slightly there.
They toss a rope and step ashore.
One's wearing a tuxedo.

Is that a film director on the pier
Beside a happy movie star tonight?
Likely he's just a passer-by
Whose wedding's at the Lido.

There goes the bridal party sweeping through
With cousins towing boys and girls. Oho,
A tiny pet. And here's the lady,
Pretty as a blossom.

An orchestra begins a lively waltz.
Hot lights are flashing down the beach a ways.
Above the buzz, the climbing moon
Is comfortably awesome.

Passing a wine and mozzarella bar,
We seek refreshment and we'd like it here.
Some bells of champagne on the spot
Infuse a light placebo.

Let's sit awhile to plan tomorrow's hours.
How shall we goody-two-shoes spend the day?
Let's think about it over there
Beside a small gazebo.

Yet microphones move closer than we thought.
They want a quote or something daft to use.
A million viewers must be bought,
And don't forget the highbrows.

You tell them we are visitors to earth
From centuries far off in future time—
So, what deodorants are good?
Ick! People shave their eyebrows?

Promptly the cameras swerve to charm
A nearby supermodel's bosom friends.
Our hearts can beat alone as one
Again. The night is open.

Bolero

Summer Moon on Calm Water

Now while moonlight unfolds bright on the world like chalk,
And Spring artlessly inks leaves to unanimous
Trees, so with unforeseen steps,
Time, being beautiful, walks where you walk,

And far voices fade out, in as the night air bends.
Speak close, Muse, of the unquenchable whirl of life.
Where's Ben Jonson? and Sappho?
Nero? *Lascaux?* Casanova's girl friends?

That far party, its laughs slide on the wind. Unbraid
Your hair, let its cologne rise in the evening air.
There. Yes. What did you say? Muse,
Tell me somehow that our minutes don't fade.

Faint whirls dimple on flat water where fish delight.
Gold clouds shine, disappear slowly behind exact
Trees. Life rushes within us.
Look how our glances devour stage fright.

And leaves curtain the moon. Shadows of hope and clay,
We grow quiet as if Leda and Zeus are near
While words tumble away, till
'I'd fall in love if we did,' your lips say.

'Such poor logic. And your musing is insincere.
But what are you? We know nothing, and yet something
Some way, somehow is so clear.
Tell me a watchword a wanderer might hear.'

'Sip small wine to a new world if you think you ought.
We walk only a while here on this earth, and soon,
Too soon... (oh, you know that).
Don't overdo. You might wish you had not.'

Full Moon, Santorini

Sunset's red nightfall descended about the horizon in deep tones,
Gilding the wave-tops that spread blue-black to the flat of the sky's rim.
East in the far dark suddenly over a hill, a balloon swelled,
Bold as a wonderstruck babe in delight cooing *Oh what a joke,* and
Drifted above high, into the silvery stars while the night grew.

The Plague, A.D. 2020

An autumn jet grinds the air overhead.
The ceiling fan seems to turn, but it is not clear.
My analog watch ticks close by my ear.
The neighbors do not speak. I rest.
A faraway radio is all that I hear.
My eyes reopen onto a different year.

For Rembrandt's Landlord, Christoffer Thijsz

I kissed a 400-year-old
lady in the art museum today,
while the guard was out
making whoopee.

She wasn't abruptly
pretty, my Lady, though she was
beautiful. Her lips were
red and pretty ready after
all those years of
no more than air.
Her hands were porcelain,
and she wore wild,
wild posies in her hair.

She had blushed a bit.
It looked as though the artist
had had an
insinuating style.

Quick

I've been writing three
  days, invisibly,
thousands of words
  in the air,
like an orchestra conductor.

  There's charisma in the air
'round you, you, you arctic fox.

  Sniff the sky with me,
look at that amusing
  moon.
My "Wate and Fate" card says
  "The sunup breeze is best,
retain it all day."

Seldom do I meet
  such a soft treading
cadenza.

Bolero, Say Hello—Nobody Is Exactly Like Toots

Blurred with beauty, the
huntress of food walks to a
market, unaware.

Blurred with beauty, the
picture of poise roams all the
aisles, busy there.

Blurred with beauty, the
muffin of sense buys from a
vendor, with no care.

Blurred with beauty, the
nimbus of Toots shops at that
kiosk, faultless, where,

blurred with beauty, a
humorous Toots jokes with a
tourist, free as air.

Blurred with beauty, the
body of Toots sways on the
C train, unaware.

Blurred with beauty, the
cupcake of charms heads for the
Five track, just aware.

Blurred with beauty, the
gift of surprise slows on the
platform, quite aware.

Zoom. Blurred with beauty,
the ginger of snap phones for
her ride, free of care.

Blurred with beauty, the
person of Toots waves from the
curb to me, aware.

Blurred with beauty, the
measure of Toots sits at my
side, beyond compare.

The Big Carpet

Unsquare, you gerrymander over all;
your fit displays your very perfect charm:
you run upstairs and down, from wall to wall,
preserving footage soft and safe from harm.

All soles receive your gentle, loving care,
as well as socks and tumbled pennies legion;
time's heels, at least won't wound or rub you bare
since throw rugs top your every trafficked region.

Your patterns, loud as Chaucer's tavern,
are woven deep and planned for hefty use,
with painted scenes from Chauvet's cavern,
commingled with laughs from Mother Goose.

Your grooming comes once each nexteen days:
a vacuum cleaner whistles till it tidies
you enough to sprawl and blithely laze
below my bouncing babies' dydies.

Then moving day to my new penthouse suite
reveals your size exceeds the terraces.
If you can't make your ends somehow retreat,
I'll rearrange you into saucy little arrases.

Boost Repeat Sales with Dactylic Studies

Well, it's a new and a wonderful world for us lyrical poets.
I've been studying old Greek fireworks: Homer. You know it's
Sure what a boulevard bard like myself needs some of to win great
Customers over. The words must be just so stress wise and load weight
Carefully, too many dactyls and I want to drown in my cocoa,
Too many two-step spondees and things shake badly like loco
Mexican jumping beans trying to cha-cha-cha. But dactylic
'Size six' booms at a suave oratorical hot foot frolic
Out in the slam po dives where a strong syncopation is hard hat.
Nobody wrote like Homer the Great! All the same if you like that
Long beat, you can deploy it in blog posts. Colleagues that know it
Well are the best.—Now maybe they'll pigeonhole me with the Poet.

Tabletop Thoughts

Luminous kitchen, confecting this morning a savory sunrise.
Silvery pots hum, apple slice wedges are brilliant as half-moons.
Saturday spoons: gold oranges, nutmeg or cinnamon, bread, drink,
Fragrant and bright. This meal is just what I needed, now. Thank you!

More Golden than Gold

Sitting in this early afternoon
Near beside you while we talk and rest,
Discussing almost nothing beyond today,
Its graceful grace, its barely headline weather,
And print-outs of inky words I like to say,
That you can also say, is one of the best
Things a friend can give, a perfect boon.

The lawn is calm today, except for that bird
Listening for worms or hoping for a tryst,
Who will see nothing busy here: two folks
Adjacent with only their paired thoughts, together
Looking at the scene, occasionally making jokes
And thinking about a rhyme that won't be missed;
Silence more golden than gold, and not absurd.

Basho's Foghorn

The frog comes with little wet feet. It sits down on the sandberg. Frog sound!

Capriccioso

Right, left, shove on the concrete as you curve along
while lights flick up to green perfectly (can't be wrong),
moves your stride like a banjo's
tinkling bells and the mind goes ding-dong,

While those traveling jets, rail or anyhoo
but hot toe on the ground—even a feather-blue
wing hang-glider or sail plane—
cannot compete with a waltz in good shoe.

Life breathes huge when you step live on a city street.
Not one citizen won't ogle; the purr is sweet.
Think growl. Eyeball around. Dance.
Nothing's as nimble as absolute feet.

Winter Full Moon

You are the valentine of my
ear. There's no other
time than when
we walked
the shining
streets of space,
and far away came finer
than candlelight, your soft soprano.

Take This Rose

Dusk's red coin in July lording the painted skies,
Drops down afternoon gold, draping a glory full
Round your shoulder this evening,
As if a spotlight has fired by surprise.

Instantaneously toppled from head to heels
I halt, savoring your molecules bright above
Small talk alchemy—halt, but
Nip tiny handsprings and little cartwheels.

When dawn's pageantry: clouds steep above waking farms,
Blinds night's audience—stars steady above, below,
Our quick-tilting disrobed earth—
Turn to me proud of your petulant charms,

Hushed, sublunar, upsetting no quantum state,
Not one subsonic wave, no combination lock—
As one woman beyond price,
Turning with elegance ever more great.

Great minds think we admire instinct, fixations, form,
Yet I know of a reason for this simple truth:
Love's own self will be remade
Freshly each day that we keep it warm.

Take this rose that I give, lovely as you deserve:
You, more lovely than all roses whose scents confuse
My poor senses with their breath—
You and this slow-beating heart, that won't swerve.

Woman: Cubiculum, House VI, 15, 14, Pompeii

Lovely, your body as pink as a seashell, a tessera image
Painted with small stones hard to efface, as you play in the water,
Splashing the delicate soft hues, chaste, a Seurat and alive, who
Bathes, chats, hiding as parts curve, always the roses and textures.

If They Want a Reason, Invite Them Too!

And went out of the bookstore to hear banners snap,
Smell soft summer on fair fields all full of folks
Who pushed money at barkers:
"Get your ticket to see the show."

Some want poems, a song sweet as a summer peach—
With heartbeats—or a faint laugh in a minor key,
Poured out careless as clock chimes
Or waltz rhythms across the dark…

—Shakespeare's sonnets be pop tunes in the mist for they:
Hamnet, Marlowe, the rose spies of Elizabeth:
So pass by with a kind eye
Posthaste, languid Procrastines—

Some want music, a dance tune just to shake their heads,
Le jazz hot, with a horn shimmy and flirty moves
While crowds sashay to steam heat
Big-band hustles and gallivant.

Some want quantum-hop big-time possibilities,
Cool-limned calculus so fine as a field of wheat.
Fresh fruit vegetable stands—hey,
Have some cucumber dips tonight!

Some bulge muscles in slow motion to heft a stone,
Some chase data or play poker or sign a book—
Lots roll strollers with babies
And do pirouettes. Meanwhile, long

Low tide surf comes to shore slowly and spreads in deep
Shade flat resonant bass canticles—dusk and star
Sparks climb into the night sky
Tall with galaxies turning far.

Song for the Grand Ole Opry—It Never Happened

I went home from work, honest as the town clock,
And there by my steps you were waiting,
My good old bad news, a wrong lemon on the rocks.
One day you'd been special when there was little to lose.
Then our eyes met. I almost fainted.
A brand new lemon zing in my salad,
My good old bad news.

You said you had gentle memories of me,
Was there time now for coffee and telephone numbers?
I said yes and lost the best part of me.
But my hopeless was gone, run off with your smile.
It was fair weather clouds and hootenanny summers,
Rose bushes and bittersweets mile after mile.
My good old bad news.

Now I wonder how we could have figured our chances:
Moonlit roads with no headlights weren't ever my style.
Would our paths ahead laugh for us and turn into dances?
You were good to spend talk with, then reality failed.
Just finding our way made the planet all right.
We'd been off to the start. Oh my, oh my, please do sleep tight.
You were the lemon wedge for my teacup,
My good old bad news.

Goalie

Bring roses, deep wine also with apples, and
Ham sandwiches too. Love rosy-fingered laughs
Right by me, her thoughtful glances
Close as a whisper—no, closer by far.

Fools know that our hearts' friendship is merely zest,
That gentle charm, verve, gusto are tidbits time
Yields flesh, that our best ways of holding
Each are like carnival volleyball as

We two exchange mind bling in a pride of day,
Your eyes to mine fair, all the most beautiful
Things crowding them when quick surprise calls
Suddenly gracefully bringing a smile.

Fools say our goalkeeping is not for aye,
But no, we share our gifts, bestowed for free,
With utter care indeed, and not lost,
Storing the measure of common delight.

Apple Tree Lean Down

   Your silhouette of leaves
among Spring's gold night,
etched under jade bright cloud
  halls, featherlike soft
to unfold, to hold, the
  moment's rounding design
  in stark future tense,
almost unmoving. I put
  these in sleepy type,
for our eyes' soft praise
  after sunset while shadows
slip and we listen
  to time slide over water,
  or when my autumn
self comes to pluck
your orchard's ripe
  slope of apples,
leaf and pale blossom now,
  these enamel days.

At the Square Dance

After *Lecto compositus* of Petronius Arbiter

I need to find roses for my love, and sweet apples.
Where can I find flowers at this time of night?
The Songs of the Auvergne have utterly seduced me,
and a goddess of love has caught me by the hair.
How can you know as I wander the sidewalks,
barefoot, half clothed, at night under the Fox Star,
every doorway or window, each fountain and coquille,
closed to me everywhere. I am condemned
to build towers like Babel, roll stones in a square,
watch cities tremble around me. Give me apples
in moonlight, a garden, flowers for her hair.
Apples with their fragrance and soft golden roses
to rest at her doorway or place on the stair.
Let her take them with laughter or burn them to ashes
with dreams of pink velvet, vanilla and clove,
doing nothing till times of thunder and ivory.

I'm condemned to bring petal storms of bright golden roses,
the Songs of the Auvergne have utterly seduced me,
a goddess has reached and pulled me by the hair
from my bed to the avenues for Eros, and her.

At a Café Nervosa Reading on Cornelia Street

The times I care the most and yet I wait:
Your chassis, warm and springy by my own,
Original equipments, up-to-date
With furnishings to make an artist moan—
The way you think! And how you sit at ease
Out there at Olympic-level spelling bees,
Where all the crowd calls out by pairs and fours
To taste ambrosial nectar unalloyed
From plashing beakers as Hephaestos pours
The steepy drink that Homer's songs declare.
Then, as you smile, my breathing slows to stare,
And if you turn away I am destroyed—
What though a hundred scribblers share my sighs
When you, my muse, stand up and greet my eyes.

And at the Writers Conference,

I went to the Old One—
Chaucer, they said, was his name.
He taught me to live on poetry and eat paper.

I said, Speak to me of God. He clapped one hand
Three times and a sunflower peeked out of his ear.
     He said,
"There are no more miracle-workers! Listen,
That is an extinct behavior pattern."
Now, Jeff Chaucer knows where it's at and how it got there.

I said to him then, Speak to me of Philosophy.
And the sunflower fell to the table, glowing a terrific orange.
My guide Geoffrey Chaucer tossed back his head and sang,
     "Said Bishop George Berkeley, looking
Through a beer glass darkly
'When a Tree Slaps the Ground
God Riffs With the Sound. Oh boy.'"

I said to my up-to-the-minute friend, Master Chaucer,
I said, Speak to me of the Meaning of Life.
And at the table where all of us lived on poetry,
A soda can winked at another soda can.
My instructor, that Canterbury author, whispered,
"You must not play two guitars at once. Ravel would
     Never approve. Don't do it."

I spoke again to the great one, I said, Speak to me of Love.
The soda cans hugged near the sunflower that was orange.
     And the connoisseur said,
"Love floats like a butterfly
     And stings like a small hymenopteran.
     Love avoids serpents.

    Love is the superstructure and the base.
    Love can be fuzzy and love is a kiss.
    Love, be a lady, tonight."

And I left Geoffrey floating about ten inches above literature,
With the soda cans running madly
In smaller and smaller circles,
    Squeaking,
While the sunflower made eyes at me.

The Earthquake and Magnetism Man

My father watched atomic bombs go off.
Say what!? He really did, you mustn't scoff.
Fifteen or twenty, the count I never knew, whatever!
There were plenty in dry Nevada and the remote Pacific
Atolls with heavy glasses and some dozen miles aside.
He showed me, his youngest child, with clearance, one day
A color photo almost big as me of one climbing orange
Mushroom after he came back from a special area far away.
At work he quietly unpacked the arcane seismograms of
Other bomb tests by people whose names I mustn't say.
A partly secret life, well spent, with strain he did not need
For a pacifist believer in the Apostles' Creed.

His first work was merely science: the earth's magnetic
Fields, its earthquakes, better buildings, its continental drifts.
Then suddenly these got interesting, and he had gifts
That no computer then made could judge for sure,
And that aged him—as I watched—too fast, as quakes
Mixed with *who did this one,* quake following quake or blast.
He didn't work alone, and I'm sure the results were treaties
That kept the peace. He was a peaceful man, a fire spotter
In danger's forest, with an American co-worker from Japan.

There's a *National Geographic* photo from '44,
Doing precision measurements to help us win that war.
Another later on the front of *Life* magazine in a crowd
Of khaki-covered men in a desert, photoed from behind,
Watching a glowing growing monster supremely loud.
Silent and angry, yet I guess he had to be rather proud
To be so trusted, working where he never expected or
Ever even wanted to work, yet had to work, measuring,
Reading, watching, when safety's silent push came
To safety's major shove.

May he rest forever in peace, and yes somehow
I hope to celebrate with him (perhaps above)
If and when we can meet and chat, and I
Can show him this tongue-tied son's
Enormous and imperfect love.

Tanglewood

    Is there music here?
Now the children of afternoon
Step the meadow. Courtly measures
      Salute twilight.

    After setting sun,
Gossips hush to muted hobnob.
Hoots and squeaks reverberate
      Soft through heaven.

    Cloudlets ride above.
How the cimbalom resolves!
Artists steady into silence.
      Hundreds listen.

    Ennui scampers out.
Closing rhythms laud the hillsides.
Time returns. Warm night's hearers
      Hurrah, and exit.

The Greenmarket

The farmers' market visits us today
with folding tabernacles near the lawn
beside the clock and courthouse on the square.
Some nearby ladies take the sunshine too,
while strutting pigeons aggravate the view
where lawyers, nannies, careful moms, compare
what vegetables and pies came in from dawn,
rain or shine, for us to buy perhaps.

The vendors grin below their baseball caps
to each as cops and idlers walk around.
The ladies drift away. It's almost four.
Still, pigeons must parade, the whole world knows.
An odd man dances through on all his toes
just like a rubber ball. And then, a score
of birds, or so it seems, swirl on the ground
beside me where a neighbor tosses bread.

The noise of cars and airplanes overhead
cannot disguise the clock bell counting five.
A seller's tent folds up. Blue shadows stretch:
broad afternoon is entering the air.
A mom with stroller shops, but now they're rare.
At half-past five, the farmers rise to fetch
what stock is left and rack it for the drive
of sixty miles to bedrooms where they stay.

Spoken at the Square Dance

```
W h e r e h o w n o w h a t
H e r e h i s h o w h a t s
E r e w h o s e w h a t h e
R e a l l y a n o n o s h e
E g o t h a w h a t h e r e
H o w n o w h a t h e r e s
A w h e r l e t h e r o h i
P s h a w h u t h y e g o s
N o w e a c h e h e h o w h
O t h a t h e y s a y w h o
W o o d i d w e l l w h e n
H i m h e r y u p h w æ t s
E g o t h a t s o g r e a t
N o t h e m s o h o w h o s
```

Analogue Beauty

Costwise, it's eBay that's good enough for me
surfing the Internet—nothing there is free.
If I want another slide rule log-log cal-
culator that delivers fast as thought,
my light-speed ready-readout pal
from Keuffel and Esser: that's where it should be sought.
My K and E, I have it still today.
So lovely! And stored not very far away.

Survivors' Club

I'm a direct descendant of the first amphibians
  who squirmed onto dry land without going back.
I'm of the alert, brave half-mammals that
  out-hustled a thousand-million dinosaurs,
    and scampered on, not glancing back.
My family is the best family of the fluffy scrappers
  who did things better, and better again:
    sometimes nicking the first stone,
      or strutting: "Follow me," parading;
Or backing up face-to-face to duck under and slash, then running,
  or maybe Gotcha now! Hah! Ah!
Sometimes giving thumbs up, staying with the wife,
  tickling the babes.
Sometimes waiting terrible as a witch growing rat poison,
sometimes living by guess and by gosh,
  good fathers, good mothers,
    never giving up, never looking back.

The survivors' house is the long house of low,
  genuine roughbrows,
  the old house of careful tricky somewhat
  sandbagger otherbrows:
  the fustest with the mostest, the quietest at the farthest,
  the most handsomest raptor on site now or never, and an artist.
The good hand hunters (slippery there),
  the rock smashers, the long ago boomerangers
  the fast-er duckers, the Ever hesitators, and the Never hesitators;
  the ancient long, long, ago I'll live (not you, sorry);
fighters, biters, sailors, fakers, takers,
  the knot-benders and big careful stackers and tailors
(Bear pelts *do* make the Man, look! Some cloth for the Lady?)
  the talkers and tellers, and sometimes liars. Quieter than trees,

Silent on toes, often with no big weapon: "That's
  one bad edge in your fist, Mister Large. R-right you are!"
  The better builders, the bandagers (relax those tense muscles,
  ma'am?), the bone-setters and bug-murderers, grrah!

The food grillers who were friends and alert. The slowly wiser
  medicine makers who stayed healthy enough, long enough.

I said some (had to be quite a lot) were good at red rock ax
  and cut work.
      Centurions, some of them, once—or archers,
        who were exactly good enough, when necessary.
And sharp ones beyond knife need, who could sometimes say,
    "Not going to argue today," and could walk away.
    They came through also,
      being beyond average with balance and bad odds there.
And there were those whose feet hurt and sat down a lot, looking,
  who made shoes or invented pliers or wrote Linear A memos,
    or hitched wagons to oxen or horses.

The survivors have had good fishers and farmers; are fifty percent
    naughty charmers;
And they numbered ten fingers, ten toes, twenty-eight nights
    a moon (seven and seven and more sevens), and winter months,
      and watched the planets go down and up and around.
They counted herds, and put down a pebble for each one born alive.

Some planted crops after bull maneuvers and studied cow thoughts
  and silly-minded sheep and chickens, and smelly goats.
Some set the chivalrous style in caves and mud and wood palaces:
  careful lassies and caring gents just about anywhere.
    Those ones who counted mostly ate good things,
      (even at need, perhaps, ancient horses).

I speculate, perhaps some of those were the off-sprout of misfits
  that did the necessary when none could figure the necessary
    or how to do it, but they did it anyway.
      And another one close by might ask,
        "I think I saw a good move there,
          yeah. Please, don't be a stranger now.—
            Care to research tomorrow's breakfast?"
Surely a few were grouchy in their time maybe, now and then.

Most were samples of wrong but right motherhood,
  wrong but right fatherhood: the ten times ten-
  thousand generations
  caring for sleepless little ones in wild weather of war,
  plague, plague after plague, with more plague, and fire;
  learning from disasters; eyes open,
Digging a few blessings from disguise, somehow.

Even a few of them drove
  open ships beyond a hundred horizons,
  with crazy wooden figures cut on the prows,
  sailed their wives and cattle through bad weather,
  rowing with no wind,
And some of these even
  swung heathen oars out over salty deep water from
  sway-bottom
  wind-rocking dragon-boats by the late low light to larboard
  on a never-a-Bible ocean, seeing the still-standing
  day in the south, —
Midnight Sun after Midnight Sun—
  all the hours from Norway to Orkney
  to Shetland to Faeroes to Iceland to Greenland
  to Newfoundland and south beyond, again and still again;
Hauling timber for mid-ocean house and home—
  Some of them.

I speak of sea captains warping tin home on
  cool ocean boat roads from lands west of Stonehenge—
  and merchants inching around the Central Sea, coasting
  from Hellespont to Ithaka, past the Atlas Mountains,
  in and out the Pillars of Herakles and the Nile Delta—
  dreaming of kings and queens high on steep Crete
  under the Dog Star.
And Phoenicians who went South from Gibraltar
  to near the pole West to East, then back North
  to the Mediterranean —

Keeping the shore in view every day, as the Egyptian papyrus
  says, and how they met the endless cold ocean river
  flowing past the world's icy bottom —

And among the thousands of thousands on this world there were
  Polynesians, and Inuits and Aleuts, and many walking to
  America in the bitter cold and dark and their own
  Midnight Sun over the Bering Straits long ago.
They went to Peru and Macchu Picchu and farther, all the way:
  Tierra del Fuego. And the first Australians;
  All those first boat crews driving to Hawaii and every
  Point south and east:
Survivors every one of them, wave watchers, star watchers,
  fish watchers. Chance takers, most very careful chance takers,
  But thoughtful and lucky too. Bravest of people.

The survivors are sometimes lucky,
  but they don't trust luck much,
  unless you call having pluck and planning, luck. Mostly,
They cobble up their own good luck,
  believing, right or wrong, with good friends
  that heaven helps those who help themselves;

that care and caution count,
that fortune favors the bold—sometimes—and
that the way of things
bears up the prepared.

And these are the ones who will laugh and worry,
  and count their blessings, and do it again,
    and again, and again—not stopping,
      not looking back.

A Wedgwood Vase

Few will find us here,
No one we would know,
And few will care who tie up their hair
With a gaudy ribbon bow,
How much I like this hour
On summer's green lawn.

It's all in how we do it,
Choosing flowers, how you bend,
The way you stand to look so grand
Until our rambles end.
Then quiet will renew it
Beyond this afternoon.

Close by, gold bottles bloom
With gusts of brut champagne
That's highly prized by the civilized
Who people dusk's terrain,
Not noting us, bride and groom,
And the moon that climbs the lane.

Bronx Cheer

Bourbaki's best bird's in the Bronx,
fleeing musical policy wonx
who lived in Manhattan
yet thought in pig Latin,
and seldom put tunes in their sonx.

Disembarking at the Poem Station

Who's this I hear of all that I have known,
Brushing past crowds of empty priceless talk?
Indeed, how sure they travel in snow or sun
Around the surface of time's nameless dream—
Those movements unforeseen in a far-off heart
That cool like raindrops before I hear them whisper
Bittersweet songs on a late Spring day—and yet,
We know our friends far off by how they walk.

Applying the Axiom of Choice

Why'd you bounce me awake here in this crowded dream,
Eyes sleek shut with the passion of an odalisque,
Silent worry in your words,
Then slam off if I try to speak?

You must know that I craved exactly a plum like you.
Didn't you know that I fold only a lady's wreath
Against me for her zoom, those
Soundless hours I drove you home?

When love swooped and we laughed, tumbling adown, our wet
Boots soft splashing the lake's ultramarine, you saw
How I hoarded your giggles,
Hot heartbeats, every angry tear.

Oh wham bam cryptogram! Did tiptoeing beauty sing,
All blossomy and close, stumbling sleepy words,
Again those thousand and one songs
From her art beyond art and arts?

Once we ambled among meadows of lawn and spice,
Trading garlands and bouquets till we stopped and stared—
And soft birds of our fingers
Fluttered up to forgive somehow.

Einstein at Princeton Reflects on the Earlier Music of France

In June 1905 when the French mathematician Henri Poincaré was 51years old, and in July 1905, Albert Einstein (then aged 26) submitted for publication identical Special Relativity velocity formulae.

Fiddling soft sounds, his bent fingers rubato
a rhapsody to rowdy humanity's world-line.
He sighs a wanderer's once-again sigh.
How many mentioners fail to follow him,

flying fast as daylight, to galactic tracts
where time turns to tar in weight-warping ways,
where vacuum condenses like rubbery jello
adjacent each sun.

He ripped the fabrics of his mourning gowns
those al-Qari'as when starbursts bit the towns.
He liked ice cream, but less the random math
of chance-filled worlds that maze a photon's path.

How many plumbed his deep blame of the planless,
how many know how he hoped beyond prayer,
'Old God may be crafty but can't be pure evil…
Does science play false? God wouldn't roll dice…?'

Pantheist pacifist, friend of the little,
silent in sorrow: a schizophrene son.
He signed a dark letter that brought wormwood and burning,
still using strange maps Poincaré had drawn.

What the Trees Told Me to Say

A light arrives. And ladders to upsway,
Each at a time, that join where sliding floors
Appear. On quiet footsteps she is there,
A girl beyond a gap no one could leap,
And she is fair. A shadow light as air
And sun in summer lanes, she slips through doors
And hallways far abroad in time and height

To hear a flourish sounding in the night.
Yet she won't trouble him that she has found,
Who sips a cup of whey—ambrosia crumbs
Strown all around—with eyes agog as day—
Who sings a name, a little chant and hums:
There's lads and ladies strolling in that sound,
And trees—and smiles while making notes to write.

Sum summus mus. ("I am the mightiest mouse."
    —Latin, anonymous)

A poem should not mean but really squawk.
Sonnets or villanelles might sweetly bite,
Horatian odes can move with music's sway,
An epic tells a tale that holds the mind,
Free verse must be like wine or else it's crap,
And Sapphics are just mush unless they snap
With extra zip, refined beyond refined;
Those haiku without frogs won't save the day,
Confucian songs might make you cry all night,
Icelandic grunts are great—like idle talk:
But, hoisting steins, the scholars praise with foam
A two hundred thirty-seven letter palindrome,
And wonder if they can get a vocal crew
To sing it out in Harvard Yard and Dogpatch too.

While Walking the Delectable Mountains

Among the ones who have foreseen the Rapture,
Those few (must I somehow join in?), might be
The hearts of some that God arranged to capture
From ancient crowds in startled Galilee
Who, listening close—as did the first Confucians
Or Buddhists near that pessimistic one—
Understood our duty amid illusions,
And shared the loaves and fishes of the Son.
Yet comes, as I ramble in these wretched pastures
Long overgrown despite their Masters,
The boom of beaten drums from other pastors.

The Number Bird

Bourbaki's best parrot could rhyme,
but preferred to spend most of its time
undisturbed in a Venn
squawking rapid Mersenne,
reciting the latest new Prime.

Literary Translations

Carmina of Horace, Book I, Number 5

What boy, tender in rose petals and perfumed damp
with balm, down in a sweet cave is cajoling you?
For whom, Pyrrha, do you tie
your hair, easily elegant,

red-gold blonde. Unprepared, oh! for the times when he
wails gape-mouthed as the gods shift with your lies and when
dark gales roughen the sea's glass—
this boy, gullible, trusting you

now, who gladdens in your glory, who hopes you will
be free always, alone, always affectionate—
he knows nothing till fortune's
false breeze turns. And the sufferers

you woo, glamorous, untried…. As for me, a vowed
thanks-pledge hallows the wall, evidence there of my
drowned clothes, given to that deep
god's vast forces, who holds the sea.

Metrical. Translated from the Latin of Horace.

Very Late, in Spring

Already the moon has gone down,
The Pleiades also flown low,
And midnight. The hours move on,
Yet I go to bed with no one…

Metrical.
Sometimes attributed to Ψαπφω (Sappho),
possibly a folksong or Hellenistic.

To a Sea Captain Dining at Ease with His Hostess

—after Ψαπφω 31
(during Sappho's exile in Syracuse, Sicily)

Equal to the gods that man seems to me there,
often face to face sitting spellbound with you,
hearing your soft laughter and beautiful voice,
   which is what truly

makes my heart shudder in my ribcage. For as
soon as I glimpse you even briefly, then no
longer can I speak, and my tongue is wholly
   broken, while fine fires

fly below my skin, and my eyes see no thing
as my ears are whirring aloud. And then sweat
trickles, trembling holds all my body, I am
   paler than straw and

seem to myself now to need little to die.
Yet I will dare everything, even though a
penniless lute player, when once I let him
   hear my voice only.

Metrical. Translated from the Greek of Sappho 31.

Let's Live!

Let's live, Lesbia! *Love,* and count at much less
than one cent all the fogeys' rumored sternness.
Our bright sun at the evening swoops, but he'll show
up gold, glowing at dawn. For you and me, though,
once our glamorous day lets fall its quick light,
we doze on evermore in endless midnight.
Give me smooches! A thousand, then a hundred.
Now the thousand again. A second hundred.
One more thousand and, oh again a hundred,
till we've smooshed a tremendous fund of kisses
by your count, and must redistribute incomes
lest some evil-eye guy'll see the spilled sums
of our purses, and injure us with curses.

Metrical. Translated from the Latin of Catullus 5.

After Sappho, Fragments 105a and 105c

I would not live life all alone, mother,
like the sweetapple blushing red on the
tip top twig that the pickers forgot—no,
they did not forget, but couldn't reach;

nor bloom wild away from my family,
like the hillside hyacinth tramped under
by shepherd men's feet, and the purple
blossom lies in the dirt, where no bee comes.

Translated from the Greek of Sappho.

A Roman Poet Describes Pompeii & Herculaneum

This is Vesuvius. Last year vine tendrils tinted the shade green,
this was where tanks overflowed, dyed with the noblest of grapes:
Bacchus preferred those hillsides to Nysae, his homeland,
recently satyrs on this peak were accustomed to dance.
Here was a residence sweeter by far than her Sparta to Venus,
Hercules put his own name here to distinguish the place.
Everything now lies immersed in dispiriting fire and ashes:
nor are the gods themselves glad to have powers like this.

Metrical. Translated from the Latin of Martial 4.44.

By the Meistersinger

Under the linden tree in the heather
is where our double bed was.
You can find there all together
lovely flowers on the grass.
By the forest in a dale,
tandaradei
    sweetly sang the nightingale.

I went walking to the meadow,
my love was waiting there before.
How he greeted me, Holy Lady!
will be my glory forever more.
Did he kiss me? A thousand times for sure.
tandaradei
    See how blushed my lips are?

Out there he'd shaped a bedstead,
very regal, all of flowers.
When anyone goes along that path,
they'll have to laugh a little laugh.
From the rosebuds well they may
tandaradei
    imagine where my head lay.

If anyone knew he made love to me,
(God forbid!) I'd want to die.
How he held me, no one, never,
ever will know, but he and I,
and one little bird,
tandaradei
    who won't say a word.

Translated from the Middle High German of Walther von der Vogelweide.

A Father Speaks to Confucius:
LunYu 1: 1; 11:26, 27

Isn't it pleasant to have practical use of the
Things you studied?—And how fine it is when an old
Friend drops by from so far off ?—
To live free and be debonair?...

...Zeng Shen's dad, who was fingering a broad harp,
Set it back with a ringing throb and rose up:
"Well, my wishes aren't like the dreams of those three."
Zhòngní asked, "Is there harm in that? You're each free.
Each just says what he wants to do in life's run."
So Zeng said, "At the season's end in mid-June
When Spring's clothing is ready, then alongside
Five or six of the company who've earned their
Grown men's caps, and with six or seven boys, I'd
Go splish-splash in the Yi, enjoy the wind near
The Rain Altars, and walk home singing songs." K'ung
Breathed, "My, my," and continued, "I'm with you, Zeng."

Translated from the original Chinese.

The Olfactory Organ

Palmström builds himself an olfactory organ
and plays von Korf's Sneezewort Sonata on it.

This begins with triplets of alpine herbs
and enchants with an acacia air.

But in the scherzo, suddenly and without warning,
in the middle of the tuberoses and eucalypti

occur the three famous passages of sneezewort
which give the sonata its name.

Each time at these hot sauce syncopations
Palmström nearly falls off his seat, while

Korf, at home, seated solidly at his workdesk,
hurls Opus after Opus onto the paper....

— Christian Morgenstern. Translated from German.

He Pictures the Brevity of His Own Life, and How Nothing Seems to Have Lived

"So! Life ...?"
    Nobody there?
Fortune's worn
my years off
Madness
hides the hours
    now

Who's strong enough
to know
where
      youth, health
fled?

Life's gone away
Memories crowd up
Evils
  walk about me

Yesterdays: done
tomorrows not yet here

today
  hurls itself
on a point

I am I've been
Ile be
  a tired
Is

Today, tomorrow, yesterday
I knot diapers
to shrouds

and endure:
a cavalcade
    of deaths.

Translated from the Spanish of Francisco Quevedo.

People from Leros

This by Phocylides. People from Leros are bad. Not just one bad, one good. *All* bad—except Procles—and he's from there too!

Metrical. Often attributed to Phocylides. Translated from Greek.

The Mannequins

Many who look to be sober, controlled, and who dress in the best threads,
 who look solid and sound, haven't a thought in their heads.

Metrical. Often attributed to Phocylides. Translated from Greek.

Pennsylvania Dutch Children's Prayer

Des Morgens, wenn ich früh aufsteh',
und abends, wenn ich schlafen geh',
seh'n meine Augen, Herr! auf Dich.
Herr Jesu! Dir befehl' ich mich. Amen.

In the morning, when I get up early,
and at night, when I go to bed,
my eyes, Lord, look to you.
Lord Jesus, I place my guidance in you. Amen.

Translated from Pennsylvania German.

Notes

"The Number Bird": Venn Diagrams

Venn diagrams can look like a group of overlapping rings (like the Ballantine beer logo) with various "items" distributed inside the loop spaces. Items in these loop spaces are distributed among the loop spaces according to their characteristics (number of legs, size, hardness, etc.). Like rain puddles, a Venn loop space may be of any shape as long as all the items in each loop space have the exactly the same collection of selected features. Each loop space is limited to a unique collection of object characteristics, and each loop space must have no boundary breaks. All items inside a Venn loop space must have an identical collection of characteristics.

Unlike puddles, Venn regions never blend, but always have firm boundaries. However, Venn "puddles" will often completely surround one or more smaller "puddles" that contains items with new characteristics not found in the larger "puddle."

Importantly, it is very common for Venn regions to *overlap* each other, and any item placed where regions overlap must have all of the features (and only those features) of every region that is overlapping there.

Red Taxicabs in Kavala Greece.

At the time of this visit in 2008, taxicabs in Kavala were painted a deep red color. Since then, Kavala's taxicabs have been repainted with the more common yellow paint found on taxis in many other cities.

About the Author

Allen Tice is an independent scholar with graduate degrees in oral literature and statistical psychology. Though his career has been teaching both in high school and college, at the same time, he has been a poet. Much of his recent work uses rhyme and meter. With most of his Greco-Roman translations, he recreates as far as is possible in English the metrical patterns of the originals, which have a subtle and beautiful rhythmic music that is unfamiliar to most American readers since rhyme was uncommon long ago. Many of his shorter original efforts use or slightly modify Greco-Roman patterns. He also translates from German, Spanish, and Chinese.

His interest in Greco-Roman poetry began with high school Latin and expanded into early Greek. At TiceWords.com, he has a usually very quiet website that mentions, among other things, some of his scholarly activities regarding the Latin poet Valerius Catullus. He lives in New York City.

www.ingramcontent.com/pod-product-compliance
Lightning Source LLC
Chambersburg PA
CBHW070512090426
42735CB00012B/2753